BOOK ANALYSIS

Written by Tara Dorrell

The Secret History

BY DONNA TARTT

Bright
≡Summaries.com

DONNA TARTT

AMERICAN WRITER

- **Born in Mississippi (United States) in 1963.**
- **Notable works:**
  - *A Christmas Pageant* (1993), short story
  - *The Little Friend* (2002), novel
  - *The Goldfinch* (2013), novel

Donna Tartt is an American writer best known for her novels *The Secret History* (1992), *The Little Friend* (2002) and *The Goldfinch* (2013). She studied at the University of Mississippi and later Bennington College, under the guidance of novelist Barry Hannah (American novelist and short story writer, 1942-2010). She comes from a deeply literary family and has a particular interest in Classics. She often looks at guilt, social class and aesthetic beauty in her work, and her writing style is verbose yet gripping as she skilfully creates characters who are intriguing in their sophistication. Tartt's reclusive nature only adds to the allure of her novels, already heightened by their beguiling and intellectual subject matter.

THE SECRET HISTORY

GREEK MYTHOLOGY MEETS *DEAD POETS SOCIETY*

- **Genre:** novel
- **Reference edition:** Tartt, D. (1993) *The Secret History*. London: Penguin Books.
- **1ˢᵗ edition:** 1992
- **Themes:** guilt, obsession, Classics, paranoia, social class, fate, alcoholism, murder

Donna Tartt's debut novel *The Secret History* had a generally positive reception, selling over a million copies and becoming widely recognised as a modern classic. It has since been translated into 28 different languages.

Narrated by one of the characters as he reminisces about his school days nine years into the future, *The Secret History* follows a group of highly intellectual students at the fictional Hampden College where they murdered one of their friends. The prologue opens with the pivotal killing, while the first half of the novel then moves back in time to build up to the event, revealing how it came about. The second half follows the mental deterioration of the remaining characters, which once more proves to have fatal consequences.

SUMMARY

A CLASSICAL KILLING

The prologue takes us to the centre of the action, Bunny Corcoran's death, which chronologically only takes place half way through the novel. From there, the start of the main body of the text introduces our narrator, 28-year-old Richard Papen, looking back to his university days and recalling the dubious morality of his time there. Richard describes his mediocre and miserable life in the fictional town of Plano, California, and his desperation to leave it and his apathetic parents behind. Upon finding a flyer for Hampden College in Vermont, he determinedly applies, and manages to secure himself a place there. Having studied ancient Greek previously, he is eager to continue it at Hampden, but is prevented by the selective Classics teacher, Julian Morrow. However, after becoming obsessed with Morrow's group of intellectuals, Richard manages to gain admission to the class when he overhears them discussing a translation in the library and steps in to help. Becoming severely isolated from the rest of the college, Richard begins to spend all his time with the elite and pretentious Henry Winter, Edmund "Bunny" Corcoran, Francis Abernathy, and Charles and Camilla Macaulay. They slowly welcome him into their fold, their friendship only growing as they spend time at Francis' country house. Bunny and Henry appear to have a particularly odd relationship, as Henry appears unable to stand Bunny, yet readily pays for his meals and possessions, and even travels on an expensive trip to Italy with him over the winter break. During this time, Richard remains in Vermont, taking a room in a warehouse that results in him nearly freezing to death; he is only saved when Henry returns from the trip early and takes him to hospital. Upon returning to Hampden, it is clear to Richard that Bunny's relationships with the rest of the group have become taut and strained. Eventually Henry recounts how the group, led by him, sought to lose themselves entirely through a Bacchanal, a wild Roman celebration, and after much experimentation with drugs and alcohol, succeeded – but killed someone in the process.

Bunny had originally been involved but was not committed enough, so they carried it out without him. When he found them returning to the house covered in blood, they told him they had hit a deer, but he nevertheless pieced together the truth upon hearing a report of a farmer's death from the same night. Furious and horrified at both their actions and his exclusion, Bunny has since been taunting and blackmailing them, hitting on their insecurities and weaknesses, like Francis' homosexuality or Camilla's gender, and demanding large financial sums, particularly from Henry. He even starts lashing out at Richard, who had no part in the Bacchanal but has become someone Bunny is jealous of. He effectively makes himself hated and a potential threat with the knowledge he holds, and so the Classics students start to plan his murder in a convoluted manner, perhaps not realising that it will actually come to pass. The lead-up to his death begins when Bunny drunkenly tells Richard what his friends had done, not knowing that he is already aware. Richard is concerned that he was only told because he was the closest person, and fears Bunny telling Julian or the police. Seeing how the risk has increased, the group, led by

Henry, push Bunny to his death down a ravine. Richard was only there by chance after going to tell them that Bunny was at a party and would not show up for his routine hike, but he then becomes complicit in the murder when Bunny does appear after all.

AFTER THE SECOND DEATH

The second half of the novel looks at the psychological deterioration of each of the remaining characters and the consequences of Bunny's death, which turn out to be deadly for the rest of the group. The strain on them is evident as a sudden snowfall means Bunny's body is not found immediately, and publicity around him and the college grows. He is initially reported missing, but the manhunt becomes an investigation once his body appears, and the Classics students have to attempt to remain inconspicuous by acting as concerned friends, taking part in the search parties themselves even though they are the perpetrators of his death. Charles deals with the majority of the questioning, and this takes a huge mental toll on him and exacerbates his alcoholism, already a common habit among both the rest of the group and the general student body. As a result, he becomes increasingly abusive to his sister Camilla, and Richard is – like with the initial murder – only semi-startled to hear of his incestuous relationship with her. Bunny's funeral is stressful and fraught with tensions on all sides; there is plenty of drinking, smoking and drug-taking to tolerate not only the funeral itself, but also each other and all of Bunny's relatives.

Arguments become common between the quintet, particularly between Charles and Francis or Henry. Camilla had been flirting with Bunny's friend and the resident drug dealer, Covey, in an attempt to find out what he had been telling the police and try to curb him somewhat. This too incites Charles' anger, alienating her further from him. While Henry seems the most indifferent to what they have done, Francis becomes paranoid and suffers a mental breakdown, resulting in him briefly being admitted to a hospital, while Richard's own alcoholism worsens, although not to the extent of Charles'. Francis and Richard discover that Julian Morrow was sent a desperate note by Bunny, written on incriminating paper from the hotel he and Henry stayed in in Italy, and detailing the first murder. Julian has yet to see the stationary insignia and so believes it to be a poor fake. In their desperation to steal the letter from Julian, who is fascinated by the mystery and aesthetic of it, Richard tries to tell Henry, who holds the letter while speaking with Julian. However, he then unknowingly leaves it insignia side up, thus exposing himself and all the others. Julian, rather than report them, instead simply leaves the college, if not the country altogether, which Henry views as both cowardly and traitorous.

DEADLY CONSEQUENCES

From there, Camilla and Henry start to live and likely sleep together, much to Charles' fury. He is arrested for drunkenly driving Henry's car, who is required to appear in court with him but fears he will let something slip to the police about the two deaths in his rage. Charles refuses to cooperate and storms out, temporarily taking shelter with Richard and Francis, but leaves after believing (incorrectly) that Richard had betrayed him to Henry. He later bursts into Henry and Camilla's room, when Richard and Francis are present, and attempts to kill Henry, instead shooting Richard in the process. Henry wrestles the gun from him, kisses Camilla and dramatically shoots himself twice in the head as the innkeeper bursts in. In doing so, he covers for Charles as the general consensus is that Richard was shot trying to prevent his suicide. Through his death, Henry also lives up to Morrow's aesthetic beliefs that the man himself betrayed.

Following Henry's death, the group falls apart, with Richard being the only one to finish his studies. Francis is forced into a heterosexual marriage to keep his inheritance after his grandfather finds out about his homosexuality and unsuccessfully attempts suicide, while Camilla becomes isolated in taking care of her grandmother. Charles loses contact with them and reportedly runs off with a married woman, while Richard remains pining for Camilla. The novel ends with a strange dream Richard has about Henry, who agrees that while he is not happy wherever he may be, neither is Richard.

CHARACTER STUDY

RICHARD PAPEN

As he is our narrator, we do not receive a detailed physical description of Richard, but know that a few of his classmates, male and female, are attracted to him. He comes from the fictional town of Plano, California, and his sense of inferiority among the other Classics students remains undiminished throughout the novel. The entire account of the events at Hampden is told by 28-year-old Richard, who is looking back to a past tinged with nostalgia, longing for a time and place where he felt like he belonged. Although Richard provides us with vivid descriptions of his friends at Hampden, who he admires for both their intellect and their aesthetic, we do not get the same detail for Richard himself. We know of his previously mundane existence, but do not receive the same commentary on his actions within the novel as we do for the other characters. This is both an advantage and disadvantage, as it means that we become intimately familiar with his thought process, but in doing so also become indifferent to any lack of morals or questionable actions. Richard is so entangled with the Classics students that he cannot help but see the events that take place from their viewpoint – he might be our narrator, yet as he was personally involved, he cannot provide a detached point of view. As a result, we too see the eccentric group's actions as entirely reasonable and plausible, and even end up rooting for them as they plot Bunny's death.

HENRY WINTER

Despite being "well over six feet" (p. 17), dark-haired, pale-skinned and with a square jaw, Henry is intimidating because of his startling intellect, rather than his physical presence. Always dressed in a dark suit and carrying an umbrella, we get the impression that he would be more suited to the reading rooms of Cambridge than the hippy Hampden College. He is the unspoken leader of the group, and the driving force behind both the Bacchanal and the murders carried out. Calculating yet charismatic, he inspires love and respect as well as fear and anger, and somehow balances being overly generous with his money (which Bunny openly exploits) with manipulating his friends throughout.

He appears to be the least affected by Bunny's death, despite being the closest to him – he thinks of it merely as a "redistribution of matter" (p. 339), and swiftly moves on to focus on the pragmatic issues, like the potential FBI investigation they face. Although Henry does not appear to lose his rationality to guilt and paranoia the way the other characters do, by the end of the novel it is clear that from the Bacchanal onwards Henry has been giving in more and more to his own desires and passions, without necessarily realising the extent of it. He longs to lose himself entirely and eventually manages it, first losing his morality in killing Bunny, then losing his own life when he commits suicide. By only allowing us to see him through Richard's eyes, Tartt makes Henry appear both alluring and terrifying.

EDMUND "BUNNY" CORCORAN

Described as sandy-haired and red-cheeked, Edmund "Bunny" Corcoran is loud, brash and "sloppy" (p. 17), always found in the same frayed old jacket despite his supposedly wealthy family background. Bunny is one of the most welcoming towards Richard when he first joins the group. As a result, Richard still feels some geniality towards him even as Bunny starts to blackmail and bully them all. Although he has developed expensive tastes and expectations, Bunny is perpetually broke and relies heavily on Henry's money for his meals and wants. Upon discovering that the group (sans Richard) had not only managed to hold a Bacchanal, but had killed someone in the process, Bunny suffers the strain of their secret. It is unclear whether he is genuinely horrified by their actions or if he simply uses it as an excuse to exploit them all; as Bunny was not involved in the original killing, we have no way of knowing if he would have taken part had he been included – or if he would have had any remorse.

FRANCIS ABERNATHY

Considered by Richard as the most "exotic" (p. 18) of the group, Francis is slender and elegant, with a shock of bright red hair and albino skin. He dresses contrastingly in a black greatcoat complete with neckties, starched shirts and pince-nez, reportedly looking like a "cross between a student prince and Jack the Ripper" (*ibid.*). One of the wealthiest of the group, it is at Francis' home that much of their time is spent, and it is there the Bacchanal is carried out. He is also openly homosexual, a fact Bunny uses to try and torment him.

Following Bunny's death, Francis suffers a mental breakdown that eventually gets him admitted to a hospital. Although he quarrels with Charles as the latter becomes increasingly violent, he continues to try and help him until the end, letting him stay in the country house with Richard, who he also maintains a decent relationship with. Ten years on, it is revealed that Francis has been forced into a heterosexual marriage with a woman he dislikes by his grandfather, in order to maintain his inheritance. He unsuccessfully tries to commit suicide, and it is at his bedside that he, Richard and Camilla meet for the last time.

CHARLES MACAULAY

If Francis Abernathy is most exotic Classics student, then Charles and Camilla Macaulay are the most otherworldly. Blond-haired and fair-skinned Charles, like his sister, dresses in the palest of colours and appears as if "from an allegory" (*ibid.*). After Bunny's murder, Charles undergoes the most drastic transformation, changing from someone "calm and quite friendly" (p. 37) to someone dangerously reckless and reliant on alcohol. Initially he is one of the most welcoming of the group towards Richard, who also notices his closeness with his sister – he cannot even remove broken glass from her leg for fear of hurting her.

However, once the murder is done, he emerges a new person driven to drink heavily by their actions. Charles takes the brunt of the interrogations with the police, and the stress of it combined with his constant drinking causes him to become more violent and alienated from the rest of the group. Richard is alarmed yet curious to discover not only his incestuous relationship with Camilla, but also his violence towards her that eventually drives her from him altogether. His fury at her leaving him for Henry, along with the guilt and trauma of the murder, is what causes him to attempt to kill Henry in the novel's climax. In the epilogue we are told Charles had run off with an older woman, a strange ending for the Charles we met at the start of the novel.

CAMILLA MACAULAY

Like her twin brother, Camilla appears pale, delicate and ethereal to Richard, usually accompanied by a cloud of cigarette smoke and air of "dark sophistication" (p. 18). She is the object of Richard's infatuation, but also of Henry's and even Charles'. As a result, it is difficult for the reader to get a grasp on her character as we can only ever see her through Richard's eyes, and he cannot remain impartial. While his involvement in the story of course affects his impartiality towards the other characters, with Camilla it simply makes another blurred female character; he finds her tempting but can rarely see beyond his desire for her. He even associates her with the goddess of the hunt, Diana (p. 61), and this motif becomes more prominent when Camilla is transformed into a deer during the Bacchanal, as the goddess Diana once did. Despite this, it is clear that Camilla is the catalyst that results in Henry's suicide although it is not her fault: rather, it is Charles' jealousy over her that excites his fury.

ANALYSIS

SOCIAL STATUS

The strongest distinction Richard feels from his friends comes from his poorer social status. He comes from a miserable upbringing in an abusive household, and upon arriving at Hampden tries to entirely reinvent himself. Rather than speak of his dull and lonely existence, he instead creates a world of "swimming pools and orange groves" (p. 5), complete with charming, if lax, parents. His acceptance into Julian Morrow's highly elite Classics course only comes as a result of this mask; the professor does not care to look beyond who he wants his students to be, and someone so clearly lacking in elegance and refinement as Richard initially was had no place in his classroom. His ruse is discovered when Henry returns from the trip to Italy early, just in time to save Richard from dying of hypothermia. While it is clear that his life is not as glamorous as he had made out, like Julian, the other students still seem to believe his stories of a sunny Californian life, seeing the mysterious, aloof boy and not the one desperate for a place to belong.

Although his friends can see through the facade Richard creates, Bunny is the only one who antagonises him about it. He knows from the start that Richard's clothing is not as high class as he tries to pretend it is, but once he starts to blackmail the group his teasing towards Richards also devolves into something more malicious. Bunny's resentment of Richard comes not from his involvement in the Bacchanal, but rather from how he feels he is replacing Bunny himself. For all Bunny's delusions of grandeur, his family have little money and do not support him, yet Bunny considers it beneath him to work. As a result, when he sees Richard, who was raised in poverty, being welcomed by the group, while he himself is becoming ever more hated, it simply increases his animosity, adding fuel to the fire.

It is Richard who is most heavily impacted by the disbanding of the Classics class, his only hope for the future being from a degree. Unlike the other remaining students, he cannot afford to take his time recuperating and not working. By the end of the novel, it appears that there has only been a little change in his circumstances; although no longer in an abusive household and with both qualifications and a job, he nevertheless finds himself back in California, right where he started. Although he may not have achieved great social advancement, the time Richard spent at Hampden has a lasting impact on him, remaining until the end "the only story I will ever be able to tell" (p. 2).

A MODERN GREEK TRAGEDY

The novel's focus on Classics is made clear early on, as it is through Richard's desire to study Greek that he meets the other five Classics students at Hampden, around whom the events revolve. Study of the Classics typically looks at the language, history, literature, arts and culture of the ancient Greeks and Romans, and Tartt scatters references to Plato, Aeschylus and Homer (among others) throughout. However, *The Secret History* has deeper links to classical literature than just references to these poets and philosophers, as the novel itself includes many of the key characteristics of Greek tragedy. When an ancient Greek audience went to see a play, it was likely that they already knew how it would end – playwrights generally reworked old and popular myths for their audience, challenging themselves to maintain the interest and amp up the anticipation when the ending was already known. Donna Tartt does exactly this when she opens *The Secret History* with a scene that should chronologically be in the middle – Bunny's death. When the main body of the story then begins, the readers are made omniscient, fully aware of where it is going and unable to do anything but continue reading as the anticipation builds.

Two crucial characteristics of any Greek tragedy were the 'anagnorisis', a moment of recognition by a character of their own (or someone else's) true nature or actions, and the 'peripeteia', a reversal of fortune for the protagonist. The initial moment of recognition for Richard is when Henry reveals the details of the Bacchanal, and the farmer's resulting death. Although Richard narrates that somehow, he "did know" (p. 181), this is the first time he is forced to confront the reality of what his friends have done. The obvious 'reversal of fortune' follows Bunny's murder, when everything starts to go downhill for the rest of the group. The manhunt around campus, the interrogations Charles and Henry undergo, Bunny's funeral and the gradual deterioration of the group's friendship, as well as of individual characters, all come as a direct result of this death.

Of course, there are many direct links to the classical world in *The Secret History*, the mysterious Bacchanal being the most obvious. However, there are more subtle connections too: even the central focus on just six of the students could be seen as a link to typical Greek tragedy, which often centred around a single family unit. Away from his uncaring parents and mediocre life in California, Richard seeks a sense of belonging among the eccentric and often pretentious Classics class, who have created their own familial bubble within the college. Richard himself is unable to disconnect his time with these unconventional students from the classical world, beginning his narration by pondering his own "fatal flaw" (p. 5), the weakness that brings about one's downfall, key to any Greek tragedy. Although Richard cites his own fatal flaw as "a morbid longing for the picturesque" (*ibid.*), it is up to the reader to decide whether it is this or some other weakness he cannot see that causes his downfall – or if it was instead caused by the Henry's hubris, or a combination of all their flaws.

LOGIC VS NATURE

The transgression of the boundaries between rational, logical thinking and giving in to nature is predominantly represented through Henry. At times it seems like even Richard's ego is being used by Henry: he proudly tells him he is "just as smart" (p. 181) as he had thought, and thus welcomes him into the group's secrets while simultaneously excluding Bunny. Despite his cool, often unsettling logic (he detachedly contemplates taking over Hampden town "this afternoon, with six men", p. 39), it is at his urging that the group attempt to carry out a Bacchanal, with fatal consequences. However, the success of the Bacchanal appears to open the door to all kinds of natural temptations: while Henry may have only discussed how take over the town, he and the others actually carry out Bunny's murder. Although to them it does appear to be the only course of action left, to the reader it can feel excessive, the sort of idea one contemplates when highly emotional, but never goes through with. The manner in which Bunny is killed also demonstrates a shift from logic to passion. While initially Henry has a convoluted plan involving poisonous mushrooms, he later writes it off as "hideously complicated" (p. 280). The plan that *is* carried out leaves far more to chance and fate, departing from the rigid rationale Henry usually follows.

Once the murder is complete, the aftermath shows how each character steadily gives in to their true nature more and more; they are no longer elegant, untouchable academics, but instead students tormented by their own unspeakable actions. While Richard himself starts to drink more regularly, Charles' alcoholism worsens alarmingly, and with it his abuse of Camilla, who eventually severs her relationship with him entirely. Henry begins a relationship with her, seemingly giving in to his desire for her, while Francis suffers a mental breakdown that lands him in hospital. The Bacchanal may have allowed them to give in to nature and a kind of carnal freedom, but killing Bunny proves to be the spark needed to amplify their behaviour until once more the consequences become deadly.

FURTHER REFLECTION

SOME QUESTIONS TO THINK ABOUT...

- How does revealing the main murder in the prologue affect how we read the rest of the book?
- Compare the different psychological reactions of the characters in the aftermath of Bunny's death.
- The Classics students try to lose themselves through sex, drugs and alcohol in the Bacchanal. To what extent is this like the lifestyle already cultivated by most of the students at Hampden College?
- In the end, Richard goes along with the murder and covers for the other students. As a latecomer to the group who is never as involved in their secrets, what do you think his motivations are?
- Henry is often seen as a contentious character, at once loved and hated by many readers. Do you think he is a good person? Why?

- How does Tartt's writing style add to the air of lethargic intellect present at Francis' country home?
- Discuss how fate features in the novel.
- Whose death has the most significance, the farmer's, Bunny's or Henry's? Explain your answer.
- What do you think is the significance of the dream Richard has of Henry in the epilogue?
- Camilla acts as a catalyst for the other characters towards the end of the novel, yet does not have as large a role. Do you think her character is limited because she is seen through Richard's eyes?

We want to hear from you!
Leave a comment on your online library
and share your favourite books on social media!

FURTHER READING

REFERENCE EDITION

- Tartt, D. (1993) *The Secret History*. London: Penguin Books.

REFERENCE STUDIES

- Cwik, G. (2013) Donna Tartt's New Anti-Epic. *Los Angeles Review of Books*. [Online]. [Accessed 6 December 2018]. Available from: <https://lareviewofbooks.org/article/greg-cwik-on-donna-tartts-the-goldfinch/#>

- Niklasson, M. (2014) *Natural Violence and Escaping Reason*. [Online]. [Accessed 6 December 2018]. Available from: <http://uu.diva-portal.org/smash/get/diva2:721310/FULLTEXT01.pdf>

- Viner, K. (2002) A Talent to Tantalise. *The Guardian*. [Online]. [Accessed 6 December 2018]. Available from: <https://www.theguardian.com/books/2002/oct/19/fiction.features>

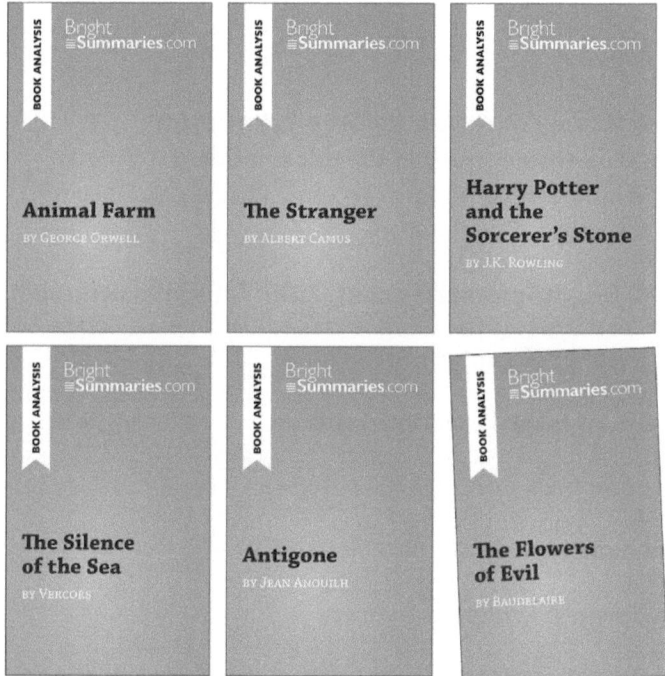

Although the editor makes every effort to
verify the accuracy of the information published,
BrightSummaries.com accepts no responsibility for
the content of this book.

www.brightsummaries.com

Ebook EAN: 9782808016438

Paperback EAN: 9782808016445

Legal Deposit: D/2018/12603/582

Cover: © Primento

Digital conception by Primento, the digital partner of
publishers.